SMALL STEPS TO SANITY

LIVING A LIFE OF PEACE, POWER AND PROSPERITY

DR. STEPHANIE L. JENNINGS

ME
WE
PUBLISHING

Scripture references are taken from the King James Version of the
Holy Bible unless otherwise noted.
Pronouns for referring to the Father, Son and Holy Spirit are
capitalized intentionally and the words satan and devil are never
capitalized.

Publisher:
More Excellent Way Enterprises
www.mewellc.com

First Edition
ISBN: 9780986423529

Printed in the United States of America.

Dedication

I solely dedicate this book to my amazing husband, best friend and partner for life, Apostle Travis Jennings, because you are my hero and the wind beneath my wings. You have always been my greatest supporter and voice of reasoning. Your strong leadership and prophetic life coaching has pushed me into destiny and I now live a victorious life in Christ. You have helped me discover the true essence of my existence. My days are filled with peace, power and prosperity, because of the small steps you've taken with me on this journey called life. Together let's allow the words from this book to break chains and bring change.

CONTENTS

ACKNOWLEDGEMENTS

To my children Travis, Briona, Daja, Destiny and David Christopher — I simply love and appreciate all that you do.

To my Harvest Tabernacle Church Family — thank you for always being supportive and loving me unconditionally. Your words of encouragement are priceless.

To all the Pretty Chics in my life (you know who you are) — your ability to rise above every challenge and work patiently with me takes great strength. I am a Pretty Chic, because you believed in the God in me.

To all of my spiritual children — thank you for your prayers and support.

FOREWORD

Do you ever find yourself leaning hard into your to-do list with the thought, "If I'm a diligent, striving workhorse, I'll get it all done," only to realize day after day, "I'll never be DONE!"?

My wife, Pastor Stephanie has the answers for life's difficult questions. As you read this masterpiece, you will discover "simple, small steps to sanity." The Father has given her this priceless revelation so we, the believers of today, can live a life of peace, power, and prosperity!

There are practical strategies in this book that believers can embrace to see greater breakthroughs in their lives. The revelation herein will add to a believer's arsenal and help them maximize and manage their moments, for maximum productivity as far as the purpose of God is concerned.

This book will give not only information but also impartation. As I read the manuscript, I felt a greater anointing and faith for prayer and strategic planning for my destiny on earth. Pastor Stephanie has tapped into an area most needed among Christian circles, and the average believer will be challenged as to maximizing his or her ministries, missions, moments, and money. Personal and corporate victories will come to those who implement these strategies.

You are about to embark on a journey of self-discovery and learn the wisdom of success. I suggest that you invest in a compact, beautiful journal that you can carry with you long after you've read this book for the first time. Throughout the book, you will find many special, challenging exercises for you to complete to make this experience more meaningful to your whole being.

Dr. Travis Jennings
The Harvest Tabernacle Church

INTRODUCTION

Are you tired of being sleep deprived, delusional, and discontented? Have you lost yourself in this rat race called LIFE? Instead of maximizing the moments, are you always fighting in the minute?

Regardless of their socio-economic status, race, class, or creed, often times women fall short of living the abundant life that God has for them, because they have become entrapped by the prison of their mind. They are now living behind the invisible bars of rejection, abandonment, and fear, being grossly victimized by "stinking thinking."

I am a firm believer that in order to change your reality, you must first change your mentality. The mind is *everything*—you are what your mind is—and your life is a reflection of the quality or state of your mind. Therefore, every change starts from the mind. It's no wonder why, as they say, *attitude is everything*!

Please understand God doesn't want us to have outward prosperity, with no inward wealth. You need to be healed and developed from the inside out. I have a saying *"deliverance can't be thought out, but it must be worked out."* This book will serve as a how-to-guide that can help you take small steps and reclaim your sanity day by day.

As a wife, mother of five, pastor, teacher, motivational speaker, businesswoman and author, it has become my life's journey and my passion to motivate women of all ages and backgrounds to reach their full potential and destiny in life. My desire is to see women fully develop into purposeful, powerful, prosperous, and productive women. I want to see them walking in the full Shalom of God, nothing broken and nothing missing.

As Naomi coached Ruth into her destiny and wealthy place, I will serve as your life coach. What Naomi and Ruth shared will be duplicated in our lives. We are not just sisters in Christ, but rather "Sistars." A unique ability is on the inside of every "Sistar," and it is time for that ability to burst out and shine bright! The world is waiting to see you shine as a light; you are not meant to be kept under the bushel but on the lampstand where your full capacity to radiate luminosity can be felt.

A "Sistar" is a believer who is committed to Kingdom purpose while conveying the truth of God's word, and consecrated for a Kingdom assignment; a commander of the morning; and a commandment follower. We as "Sistars" are bright, glowing lights in the earth realm, with God's grace upon our countenance and His unmerited favor flowing in our lives. Now is the time to shift your mentality and change your reality, and as well shift your mobility, so you can walk into possibilities. Being female is not equivalent to being weak; we carry enormous power to perform. There are no bounds to what you can do.

Small Steps to Sanity, as explained herein, will inspire, encourage, and propel you to your place of fulfillment where you will leap beyond your limitations, dream beyond your means, and achieve astounding acquisitions. You will be transformed, thrust into greatness, and taught the necessary steps to reclaim your sanity. This inspirational guide will provoke you and arouse cathartic conversations to bring about spiritual enlightenment, renewal, and healing. Feel free to share this guide with your friends and have topical discussions among yourselves. I know it will be a blessing to you and yours.

As you go through each chapter, you will find *Daily Exercises for Empowerment* and *Daily Prayer* that will help you apply the theme of this book to your life, and you will be able to track results as well.

Once again, be ready for a dramatic change from inside out...

Dr. Stephanie L. Jennings

SMALL STEPS TO SANITY

1

DISCOVERING
God's Plan for
Your Life

> *"What we are is God's gift to us. What we become is our*
> *gift to God." ~ Eleanor Powell*

Have you ever asked yourself why you are here and what your purpose is? Have you ever felt as if your life has no value or significance in the earth? Be encouraged! God has a purpose and a plan for you. His plans for you are to prosper you and not to harm you. God's design and purpose for you were predestined and foreordained before the foundations of the world.

However, you must come to discover and understand your assignment in the earth. What is God's idea for your life? For what purpose did He create you in the first place? After all, you did not just happen to be—His creating you was deliberate, as it was for a purpose. Who did God design you for in the Kingdom? When you do not have an understanding of God's purpose for your life, you become a product of circumstances or your environment, and a resource for Satan's agenda. You would begin to operate like a deer caught in the headlights, and this may lead to disastrous decisions that can alter your destiny.

Remember that all things work together for good to them who love God and who are called according to His purpose (See Romans 8:28). Nothing will work together for your good until you understand His purpose! Invariably, you're in control of what becomes of you— so revelational knowledge is important. Many are the plans in a man's heart, but it is the Lord's purpose that prevails (See Proverbs 19:21 NIV). You must identify your Kingdom purpose! *"For I know the thoughts that I think toward you, saith the LORD, thoughts of peace, and not of evil, to give you an expected end"* (Jeremiah 29:11).

You Have a Unique Purpose

Imagine a drawer full of silverware. They all share the same common goal, which is to serve as eating utensils. Yet each piece is created distinctively different and has a unique purpose toward the common goal. The knife cuts the food into smaller portions making it easier for the food to be consumed. The fork has the ability to pierce solid foods that cannot be scooped up. The spoon has the ability to scoop soft foods that cannot be pierced. The serving spoon can scoop larger amounts than the tablespoon or teaspoon. The teaspoon can fit into smaller areas that the serving spoon can't reach. The butter knife is not as sharp as a steak knife but it can smooth condiments onto food without tearing the food.

The point is that each utensil has a unique purpose, but they all work toward the same goal. Each utensil knows its purpose, so there can be no confusion or misleading as to what it has been designed to do. I've never seen a knife try to function as a spoon! Think of how disastrous it would be if you attempted to eat ice cream with a steak knife!

God wants to be glorified in the earth through you. Always remember that being different gives opportunity for your uniqueness to shine; so always be *you* on purpose. Never try to be like someone else. No matter your race, background, challenges, or physical conditions, you are the only original of yourself—there is none like *you*. Even your adversities and extremities are only opportunities for God to be glorified. Remember, God will not put more on you than you can bear.

Purpose versus Your Problem

Everything you have gone through is only there to strengthen and mold you—to conform you to His image. As you face trials in your life, don't focus on the problem; focus on the solution. After every trial, there is glory. Jesus was able to endure the cross because He was focused on the joy that was set before Him—His purpose (See Hebrews 12:1-3). Only God Himself can tell why PURPOSE sometimes hides behind suffering, pain, or a specific challenge.

Apostle Paul had a similar experience, and said, God *"comforteth us in all our tribulation, that we may be able to comfort them which are in any trouble, by the comfort wherewith we ourselves are comforted of God"* (2 Corinthians 1:4). Therefore, whatever may be your problem, focus on God's glory, which shall be revealed when you come out of the situation. Remember that the suffering you are presently experiencing cannot be compared to the glory that shall be revealed later on (See Romans 8:18).

Your momentary troubles are achieving an exceedingly greater purpose in you (See 2 Corinthians 4:17). Focus on the lesson that is to be learned so that you don't repeat the same scenario. What you want to avoid is falling into a cycle of defeat. Understand that with each trial you come through, more of the *real* you emerges, that is, the "you" that God intended! With every experience, there is a lesson to be learned, not just for you but also for someone who will come after you.

Turn your misery into ministry—as Paul did to the Church in Corinth. Turn your pain into purpose. Don't throw in the towel in the midst of the storm, for who would have known if you have come to the Kingdom for such a time as this and for this very purpose?

Remember that your purpose changes with seasons. As you mature and examine each season in your life, you will begin to understand the purpose of every experience, and how all the pieces thereof fit together. You are a masterpiece in the making.

God is working on you; you're a semi-finished product. So be patient in the hand of the Potter, though it's not easy to get broken (by challenges) and be molded again into another vessel as seemed fit in His view.

> **Mental Note to Self:** Every life experience has a GOD PURPOSE attached to it, and I was created on purpose for a purpose. My experience is not who I am, it's only what I've been through. *"We are assured and know that [God being a partner in their labor] all things work together and are [fitting into a plan] for good to and for those who love God and are called according to [His] design and purpose"* (Romans 8:28 AMP).

Understanding your purpose and assignment in God brings about personal sense of fulfillment in life. When you are fulfilled, you will gain a satisfactorily high level of life. You will begin to live the God kind of life. If you don't know who you are, take a shot at knowing God through His word to you. You can't find purpose apart from Him.

> *Before I formed you in the womb I knew [and] approved of you [as My chosen instrument], and before you were born I separated and set you apart, consecrating you; [and] I appointed you as a prophet to the nations.* (Jeremiah 1:5 AMP)

◆

Daily Exercises for Empowerment:

One of the devil's devices is to distract you from your purpose with negative thoughts and images of yourself. For instance, if allowed, he can beat you down through low self-esteem or lack of confidence—the "I can't" mentality.

The devil wants to keep you from understanding your purpose in God. He often achieves this by keeping you focused on past hurts, past failures, and past disappointments. Counter-attack those negative thoughts and images, using positive thoughts and images.

1. Change your focus. Rather than think about the things you have not accomplished or the mistakes you've made in life, write a list of all the positive accomplishments you have achieved and the good things you have done that you are proud of.

Read this list daily and set a goal to add another accomplishment daily, weekly, or monthly.

Today, I accomplished...

_____

_____

I am most proud of...

_____

_____

2. Challenge yourself. Think of something that you told yourself you could not do because of fear or past failures or insecurity (low self-esteem). Maybe it is writing a poem or reading in front of an audience. Whatever that thing is, try it! Empower yourself!

Today, I will...

_____

_____

3. Treat yourself. Get dressed and treat yourself to a matinee, a sundae, a walk in the park, a trip to the art museum, a new book, a massage, a facial care, a manicure, a pedicure, or whatever will relax you and make you feel good (and is in your budget)!

Today, I treated myself to...

_____

_____

4. Change your routine. For one week, turn off the television and try something different that you normally would not do. Step out of the box! Get involved in ministry! Exercise! Learn a new language! Find out what gives you a sense of fulfillment!

Today, I changed my routine...

_____

_____

5. Develop a relationship with God! Read scriptures in the word of God pertaining to destiny, faith, and purpose. Write down every prophecy concerning your destiny and purpose and read them regularly so that you will remember what God has purposed for you and that you may be able to fight a good fight in this spiritual warfare against your destiny and purpose!

What did God say about me?

_____

_____

6. Create a Mantra. You are on your way to living a life of peace, power, and prosperity.

This journey in discovering life's purpose has been great. It is my belief that your experience has created your life's slogan. Take this time to write a statement that explains and encompasses who you are and where you're going.

What best describe me?

_____

_____

◆

Daily Scripture Reading: Exodus 9:16, Psalm 57:2, Psalm 138:8, Proverbs 19:21, Isaiah 49:1,5, Isaiah 55:11, Mark 9:23, Romans 8:28-29, Ephesians 1:3-5, 9, 11, 17-23, Philippians 1:6, Philippians 2:13, Philippians 4:13, James 1:2-4

◆

Daily Prayer: Father in the name of Jesus, I thank you for creating me in your image and in your likeness. Today, I accept and partner with your will for my life. I decree and declare that my identity is no longer in a crisis, and my purpose is not confused. Today, I fall in alignment horizontally and vertically with your will. I embrace your plans, purposes, and promises spoken over my life. I pull down the strongholds of fear, doubt, and unbelief. I decree and declare that the eyes of my understanding has been opened; therefore, I now see my pain as purpose, my problems as potential glory moments and my past as a platform—a steppingstone for advancement. I embrace the confidence that you have given me according to Philippians 1:6 and I praise you in advance for the victory that awaits me.

2

DEVELOPING
and Maintaining
a Balanced Life

> *"Howbeit this kind goeth not out but by prayer and fasting"* (Matthew 17:21)

The spiritual life of a Christian is a function of several factors, which are required for them to be victorious in this world. God doesn't want His children to be weaklings, so He's got certain principles for them by which spiritual muscles can be developed. With these, strength, stability, and balance can be assured. Here, we want to consider one of the criteria to developing and maintaining a balanced life, which is prayer.

Prayer Defined

Prayer is more than having a friendly dialogue with God. Prayer is agreeing with heaven concerning [and in pursuit of] God's will in the earth. I once heard the late Myles Monroe say, "Prayer is simply getting heaven involved in earth's affairs."

When you pray, you will bring heaven down to earth; and when heaven kisses the earth, the essence of the Kingdom will be enforced, and the will of God done. Therefore, prayer is partnership with God as to His will for the Church and the earth.

> *Confess your faults one to another, and pray one for another, that ye may be healed. The effectual fervent prayer of a righteous man availeth much.* (James 5:16)

> *Therefore, confess your sins to one another [your false steps, your offenses], and pray for one another, that you may be healed and restored. The heartfelt and persistent prayer of a righteous man (believer) can*

accomplish much [when put into action and made effective by God—it is dynamic and can have tremendous power]."(James 5:16 AMP)

The word *effective* means to prevail, to obtain victory or success, or to produce the desired result. Effective also means producing the power to bring about a result. There are three key terms that stand out in this definition. Desire and power! You must have a desire when you pray. There is a world of difference between desire and wish. If you wish it, you won't go far with God. But if you have a desire, you will get His attention. Why? A desire is something that gets the whole of your heart; it consumes your thought. An element of *passion* is in a desire.

Therefore I say unto you, What things soever ye desire, when ye pray, believe that ye receive them, and ye shall have them. (Mark 11:24)

Moreover, your prayers must be mixed with faith! Lastly, your prayers should result in the thing you desire or the power to bring about what you desire. When your prayers are mixed with desire and faith, you are armed with tremendous power!

Another key term in James 5:16 is *fervent*. Fervent means marked by eagerness and intense passion in pursuit of something. That suggests to us that when you have a desire, your prayer will be fervent; if you only wish for it, you won't be serious even if you assume a prayer posture before all men. When you pray, you must pray as if you are in pursuit of your desire. You must have passion. To pursue means to overtake, capture, accomplish, seek, work, or chase something. For example, you may desire deliverance for your child or healing for yourself. When you pray, you have to pursue your healing, seek your deliverance, and capture your prosperity. You have to chase it. You have to work for it. You have to overtake it. You have to pursue it with your whole heart! That's a desire, which is characterized by tenacity, fervency, and doggedness!

The Amplified Bible says that *"continual prayer makes tremendous power available [dynamic in its working]."* Dynamic means marked by continuous and productive activity or change. Effective prayers have the power to produce action or bring about a change in your life!

Living a life of balance is not farfetched when prayer becomes a part of your DNA. Women, you are stronger than you think and remember you can do all things through Christ that gives you strength. Don't be afraid to carve out time in your daily schedule to be refueled in God's presence. Always remember to say a little prayer and it will release heavenly assistance in your earthly affairs. Give God the license to step into your situation and shift the outcome. It is my belief that when you take God out of the driver seat of your life, you become responsible for any accidents along the way. Heaven is waiting on your partnership to bind and loose.

Elements of Prayer

Now, we would like to look into some of the virtues that

make up a fervent, passionate, effective prayer.

1. **Binding and Losing.** Binding and loosing is a way to take control over satanic activity and territorial spirits. Binding or loosing is a contract in the realm of the spirit that establishes real authority. Remember God gave the earth to the sons of man, but Satan is the prince of the power of the air, according to Ephesians 2:2. Even though Satan has *some* authority, always remember you have *the* authority—absolute dominion power—through the power of attorney received from Jesus to whom all authority in heaven and earth has been given. The Bible calls us kings and priests unto God (See Revelations 1:6). This means that when you bind satanic activity and territorial spirits, you strip the enemy of all legal authority. Satan and his cohorts have no choice, but to evacuate. I love the conversation God had with Job when he was complaining about his situation.

    > *And have you ever ordered Morning, 'Get up!' told Dawn, 'Get to work!' So you could seize Earth like a blanket and shake out the wicked like cockroaches? As the sun brings everything to light, brings out all the colors and shapes, The cover of darkness is snatched from the wicked—they're caught in the very act!* (Job 38:12-15 MSG)

    Always remember the power is in your mouth therefore, STOP COMPLAINING, and START

COMMANDING. In the words of my husband, Apostle Travis Jennings, "GET THAT LIFE UP OUT OF YOUR MOUTH!"

2. **Effective Praying.** When there is no prayer, there is no power. As women of God, we have to always pray, even if it means that we have to carve out time in our day for prayer to make it a priority. Consider these three points when praying.

    a. **Pray without ceasing.**

- Everywhere you go, carry God with you—talk to Him in your heart and listen for His voice. Walk in God-consciousness every day, everywhere—on the street, at the park, in the woods while hiking, in the bathroom, in the kitchen...

- *"Pray in the Spirit on all occasions with all kinds of prayers and requests. With this in mind, be alert and always keep on praying for all the saints"* (Ephesians 6:18 NIV).

- *"Pray continually"* (1 Thessalonians 5:17 NIV).

- *"Pray with power, but you, dear friends, build yourselves up in your most holy faith and pray in the Holy Spirit"* (Jude 1:20 NIV).

b. **Plan to pray.**

- Be determined to pray. Set a time of prayer to meet God daily. We often call this a Quiet Time. But then, after having done that, don't think that communion with God is over for that day. Switch to point 1 above (it's neither location nor time-based).

- Keep yourself consecrated and position yourself to pray. *"The end of all things is near. Therefore be clear minded and self-controlled so that you can pray"* (1 Peter 4:7 NIV).

c. **Prioritize.**

- Naturally, we are all encumbered with the cares of life. We usually have a long to-do list for the day. Until you give a high priority to prayer, you won't pray. And even if you do pray (out of a routine mindset), you won't spend a quality time on it. You know the value of a thing by the amount of time devoted to it. Check it out!

3. **Fasting for Purpose.** As a powerful complement to prayer, fasting is a great discipline that brings about balance in the life of a believer. Firstly, let's look at the definition of fasting. It is abstaining from food or any other activity for a spiritual purpose.

There are three types of fasts:

- *Traditional fast* - it's a practice of abstinence from food consumption only. Here, you won't eat any food over a specific period, maybe hours, or days.

- *Absolute fast* - this involves abstaining from food and water. I don't recommend this unless God has led you.

- *Partial fast* - it deals with restricting yourself from pleasurable things (e.g., no meat, no sweets, no TV, no social media). When you deprive your flesh of its longings, its power weakens (your flesh dies), and your spirit man is strengthened. Whatever you feed—flesh or spirit—will take the lead in your life!

A word of advice: if you are going to abstain from food for several days (for example, seven days), make sure you begin to drink water from the third day, every evening, until you finish the race, so to say.

Biblical Case Studies

Let's consider some biblical examples of people who had the power of prayer and fasting, and who got tangible results.

1. **Daniel's Prayer.** In Daniel 9 and 10, we find that Daniel sought the Lord by prayer and fasting. Daniel

fasted for three full weeks. Because of Daniel's prayer and fasting, God first sent Gabriel, the messenger angel (Daniel 9:21-27), to give him wisdom, skill and understanding on his request. Then God sent Michael to withstand the King of Persia on behalf of Daniel (Daniel 10:10-21). By virtue of Daniel's prayer and fasting, God came in response to his words. *"Then said he unto me, Fear not, Daniel: for from the first day that thou didst set thine heart to understand, and to chasten thyself before thy God, thy words were heard, and I am come for thy words"* (Daniel 10:12).

Lessons to Learn

- Fasting gives us the enabling power to chasten ourselves! To chasten means to correct and purify; to prune of excess, pretense, or falsity; to cause to be more humble or restrained; or to subdue. Fasting empowers us to rule our own human spirit (fleshly desires and lust).

- Prayer releases the wisdom of God to handle distressing situations! God will give you understanding in the midst of your storm.

- Prayer coupled with fasting moves God to come to your aid as a consequence of and in response to your words! Consequence means importance with respect to the power to produce an effect. In other words, your prayers coupled with fasting are important, powerful, and can produce an effect.

- God will dispatch angels to fight against every principality (a territory governed by a prince or chief demons) in your life!

2. **Esther's Fast.** In Esther 4:16, we find that Esther called for a fast among all the Jews in Shushan as she prepared to go before the king to petition for the deliverance of the Jews. In the next chapter, we find that when Esther came before the king, she obtained favor in his sight. We also find that God gave Esther wisdom and a strategy to fight against Haman, her adversary, on behalf of her people.

Lessons to Learn

- Fasting brought a nation together and was the predecessor to the reality of the deliverance of the Jews!

- Fasting will set you up to obtain favor with God and with men in high places! Fasting will bring you into favor with men who have the power, influence, and ability to help you fulfill your God-given assignment.

- Fasting released the wisdom of God and a strategy to fight against the enemy (prophetic plans).

3. **Solomon's Prayer.** In 2 Chronicles 7, Solomon devoted himself to prayer. He summoned a solemn assembly when he completed the Lord's house and dedicated it to God. Because of Solomon's prayer, God sanctified the house of the Lord to Himself as a house of sacrifice and declared that His name and His eyes and His heart would be there perpetually. God declared that if the people would humble themselves and pray, then He would hear from heaven, forgive their sin, and heal their land.

Lessons to Learn

- Prayer will produce miracles; fire will come down from heaven and will cause the glory of the Lord to fall upon your household or local church (2 Chronicles 7:1).

- Prayer will cause God to choose you for Himself (to sanctify you and set you apart for His purpose). Prayer with fasting gives meaning and purpose to a person's life.

- God's ears will be attentive to your prayers and He will hear you, He will forgive your sins, and He will heal your land (your finances, your prosperity, your home, and your health).

- God will put His name upon you, and His heart will be with you perpetually (everlasting, continuing forever).

4. **Anna's Prayer and Fasting.** In Luke 2:36-40, Anna was a prophetess, a prophetic *birther*, who served God with fasting and prayer night and day, giving thanks and praise to God. Her determination and dedication gave her a direct and clear focus on the assignment of preaching Christ to all who desired redemption.

    ### Lessons to Learn

    - Fasting and prayer will bring revelation of who Christ is.

    - Fasting and prayer will birth out praise.

    - Fasting and prayer will bring about deliverance and redemption for yourself and others.

5. **Jesus' Miracle.** In Matthew 17:14-21 (also Mark 9:17-29), Jesus' disciples were unable to heal a boy possessed with a demon. Jesus rebuked the demon and the boy was cured. When asked, He told the disciples that the reason they were unable to cast out the spirit was their lack of faith; but not faith alone — this kind cannot go out except by prayer and fasting.

    ### Lessons to Learn

    - The power to cast out demons can only come from prayer and fasting.

    - Prayer and fasting must be mixed with faith in order to be effective.

- Prayer and fasting empowers your words (with official authority or legal power to take effect). Even demons will respond to your words when they recognize the power of prayer and fasting behind your words.

Daily Exercises for Prayer and Fasting:

We see from the given biblical examples that the combination of fasting and prayer is a way to humble ourselves before God, and seek Him for direction, comfort, help, strength and His will. Prayer and fasting allows us to create a space and moment of serenity around us. This stillness and peace of His presence brings undisturbed joy and the full Shalom of God upon us—nothing broken and nothing missing. According to Hebrews 4:16, *"Let us therefore come boldly to the throne of grace, that we may obtain mercy and find grace to help in time of need."* I've once heard Bishop I.V. Hilliard say, *"Repetition is the breeding ground for breakthrough."* If a balanced life is going to become a part of your DNA, you can achieve that with a life of prayer and fasting. Below are daily regiments I've provided to help you win in this journey called *life*. Once you add these small steps to your daily routine, a victorious life is inevitable.

Keep a prayer journal. This will help you stay focused, consistent, and become effective in prayer. Record your prayers and the outcome of such prayers.

_____

_____

Keep a fasting journal. What type of fast did you do and what were you fasting for? How long? What was the outcome of your fast?

_____

_____

———————— ◆ ————————

Daily Scripture Reading: Matthew 17:14-21, Mark 9:17-29, 2 Chronicles 7:1, Esther 4:6, Daniel 9:21-27, Daniel 10:10-21, Isaiah, James 5:16, Mark 11:21-24, Matthew 6:33, 1 Timothy 2:1, Proverbs 16:3

———————— ◆ ————————

Daily Prayer: Father God, in the name of Jesus, first of all, I want to say thank you. I thank you because this is the day that you have made and every day, new mercies I see. Today, I submit to your word in Romans 12:1 and present my body as a living sacrifice that is holy and acceptable unto you, my God. I bind all spirits of worry, confusion, and chaos in my life. I bind prayerlessness, fatigue, fear, and frustration. I bind burnout, including loss of energy and concentration. Today, I align myself with your word and your will. I stand on the strength of Proverbs 16:3 and I put you in charge of my work, so that what you've planned for my life will take place. As from today, I walk in great confidence that everything I have asked according to your will has been done!

SMALL STEPS TO SANITY

3

DEMONSTRATING
the Heart
of a Worshipper

> *And God saw that the wickedness of man was great in the earth, and that every imagination of the thoughts of his heart was only evil continually. And it repented the LORD that he had made man on the earth, and it grieved him at his heart.* (Genesis 6:5-6)

As born-again believers and as women who are emotional beings, we must understand that our hearts must be purged and purified daily so as not to grieve and sin against God. Today, it's unfortunate that many Christian underestimate the danger of sin—they often excuse their sinfulness, thinking that they can get away with it. Yes, God loves you, but He doesn't condone iniquity. In agreement with the Word, let's call sin what it is—sin, nothing more.

The Origin of Sin

It all started with Lucifer who was overtaken by pride and rebellion, and then decided to dethrone the Most High God. He was the father and mother of sinfulness that has ravaged humanity for centuries. He was Lucifer, but became Satan because of sin. So he is a perfect example of the crippling effects of iniquity in the heart. *"Thou wast perfect in thy ways from the day that thou wast created, till iniquity was found in thee"* (Ezekiel 28:15).

God considered Lucifer as a perfect creature in every way until iniquity was found in him. His iniquity disconnected him from the will of God and caused him to forfeit the plan of God for his life—he was ejected from heaven. In his wrath, he later went to deceive man—Ada and Eve—to rebel against God. Since that day, iniquity has dominated all the generations of man. That's why everybody that's been born into this world must be *born again* to escape the damning penalty of sin.

Forms of Iniquity

Iniquity can manifest in various forms, and these include bitterness, offense, unforgiveness, anger, rebellion, idolatry, envy, lust, gluttony, resentment, or pride. All these things originate from the heart. Whatever is in your heart can either cause you to be blessed or ultimately defiled! We must understand that Lucifer was once an anointed cherub until iniquity was found in him and he was cast out of heaven! You don't want to miss out on the Kingdom because of an impure heart! So, get that sin out of your heart.

The Danger of Iniquity

Having stated some of the forms by which iniquity manifests in our lives, let's look into what will become of us if we allow sin to reign in our mortal body.

- **Hindered Prayer**

When our hearts are filled with iniquity (inward sin), our prayers will be hindered. The word of God tells us that if you regard iniquity in your heart, the Lord will not hear you (Psalm 66:18).

Isaiah 59:2 says that your iniquities have separated between you and your God, and your sins have hid His face from you, that He will not hear.

- ## Spiritual Deadness

As far as the New Covenant is concerned, Jesus came to give us abundant life (John 10:10), but the devil is all out to *kill* us. Since you're born of God, you carry His seed, and His seed constitutes His nature. The devil is looking to destroy the seed of God in you, and his tactic is to entice you, to sin against your God. Whatever may be the case, always remember that iniquity is a poison— like a deadly virus, it can infect the heart with moral decadence, and subsequently kill your potential, destiny, and purpose in life. As Joseph did, we must flee from sin; otherwise, it will rob us of our virtue and worth as children of the Kingdom.

- ## Epidemic

One thing the devil wants you to believe is that iniquity is just a norm in humanity. He often says to our mind, "You have your life to live, why should you bother about anybody. After all, it doesn't affect them in any way!" That's a lie. Iniquity does not only affect you but also it spreads like a virus and infects someone that you have influence over, thus creating the stance that can kill his or her potential and destiny. Only Adam and Eve sinned in the Garden of Eden, but that sin is being passed down from generation to generation. Similarly, the iniquity in Lucifer infected a third of the angels in heaven. God created you so you can make positive impact on humanity, and not to complicate the pollution in this world. Don't let the devil make you an agent of his deadly mission on earth.

Developing the Heart of a Worshipper

Jesus once stated that those who serve God must worship Him in spirit and in truth. The only part of you that God asks for, and needs, is the heart. To you, He says, "Child, give me your heart." Your heart is the seat of your life. When the Lord gets it, He's got all of you; consequently, He will be happy to be with you and show Himself to you.

Matthew 5:8 (AMP) tells us that *"blessed (happy, enviably fortunate, and spiritually prosperous— possessing the happiness produced by the experience of God's favor and especially conditioned by the revelation of His grace, regardless of their outward conditions) are the pure in heart, for they shall see God!"* One must prepare the heart to seek God (2 Chronicles 30:19).

Steps to Having a Yielding Heart

1. Guard your heart. Why? As stated earlier, the heart is the core of one's being. When it gets sick, everything becomes sick. For instance, your attitude is a reflection of your heart. So, *"keep thy heart with all diligence, for out of it are the issues of life"* (Proverbs 4:23).

2. Hide the word of God in your heart. If indeed you've been born of the word of God—the incorruptible seed of God—you can only survive by living on the Word. Since you were set free by the Truth, you need the Truth to remain free. *"Wherewithal shall a young man cleanse his way? by taking heed thereto according to thy word. With my whole heart have I sought thee: O let me not wander from thy* commandments. *Thy word have I hid in mine heart, that I might not sin against thee."* (Psalm 119:11).

In addition, the Word of God has a purifying effect on the soul. See the following scriptures:

- Now ye are clean through the word, which I have spoken unto you. (John 15:3)
- That he might sanctify and cleanse it with the washing of water by the word. (Ephesians 5:26)
- For the word of God is quick, and powerful, and sharper than any two-edged sword, piercing even to the dividing asunder of soul and spirit, and of the joints and marrow, and is a discerner of the thoughts and intents of the heart. (Hebrews 4:12)

3. Forgive! When you turned God after having heard the Gospel of salvation, you were forgiven of all your sins. God expects us to forgive those that might offend us.

And grieve not the Holy Spirit of God, whereby ye are sealed unto the day of redemption. Let all bitterness, and wrath, and anger, and clamour, and evil speaking, be put away from you, with all malice: And be ye kind one to another, tenderhearted, forgiving one another, even as God for Christ's sake hath forgiven you. (Ephesians 4:30-32)

4. Ask God to cleanse your heart daily. *"Create in me a clean heart, O God; and renew a right spirit within me"* (Psalm 51:10). The only way to cleanse yourself from iniquity is to first confess your faults and then plead the blood of Jesus upon your spirit, soul, and body.

5. Pray and fast from time to time. Jesus said, and He's saying it now, *"Watch and pray that you may not fall into temptation."* Temptation will come; you only have to resist it—you don't have to fall into it.

———————— ♦ ————————

Daily Exercises for Purification:

If you have taken offense or have bitterness in your heart toward God because of the struggles that you have faced in your life, repent to the Lord, and ask for forgiveness.

James 1:2 (AMP) tells us to consider it wholly joyful whenever we are enveloped in or encounter *"trials of any sort or fall into various temptations. You must understand that trials come to prove your faith and produce endurance. But you must let patience have her perfect work that you may be perfect and entire, wanting nothing"* (James 1:4).

Have faith in God and trust that He will not put more on you than you can bear. Trust that God knows what He is doing and do not take offense at your sufferings, for Christ suffered for you (See Matthew 11:6, Luke 7:23).

Now, write down the names of every person who has ever hurt you (mother, father, siblings, former pastor, former boss, husband, ex-spouse, the one who raped you, the one who molested you, etc.). Forgive each person listed—say it aloud (say the person's name and what the person did that hurt you). Once you have forgiven every person on the list, tear up the list and flush the torn paper in the toilet or burn the pieces of paper in the fireplace.

Bid hurt, bitterness, envy, pain, and unforgiveness goodbye as the torn pieces of paper flush down the toilet or burn in the fire. It is imperative that you say each person's name out loud so that you and the devil will know that you have forgiven them just as Christ has forgiven you and that you no longer hold on to the pain anymore.

WARNING: This exercise can only be effective if you are completely honest with yourself. Sometimes we fool ourselves by thinking that saying the words 'I forgive you' means that we have truly forgiven someone in our hearts. If you are unsure whether you should add a name to the list, try this test: if you say a person's name or mention a situation and tears fill your eyes, your spirit becomes heavy, you feel anger or confusion, or your heart skips a beat, then you have not completely forgiven that person or situation.

p.s. Make sure your name is on the list! Self-condemnation can be a silent killer!

I forgive…

_____

_____

Daily Scripture Reading: Deuteronomy 30:6, Job 3:20, Psalm 19:14, Psalm 24:3-5, Psalm 78:36-38, Psalm 86:11-

13, Psalm 101:4, Psalm 125:4, Isaiah 59:2, Matthew 15:18-20, Acts 8:21-23, Romans 6:12-19, 2 Corinthians 7:1, 1 Thessalonians 3:12-13, 1 Timothy 1:5, 2 Timothy 2:21-22, Titus 2:14, Hebrews 10:21-22, 1 Peter 1:22

———————— ♦ ————————

Daily Prayer: *Father God, in the name of Jesus, create in me a clean heart and renew the right spirit on the inside of me. Today, I rend my heart and not my garment. You are the giver of life and the master of my soul, so now heal my mind and mend my broken heart. Let your saving power rise upon me and bring healing to my soul. Satan, you are no longer lord over my emotional structure. I render you powerless and helpless, because I walk in my authority according to Luke 10:19, which says, "Behold I give power to trample upon serpents and scorpions and over all the power of the enemy." I bind the spirit of rejection, bitterness, anger, abandonment, and malice. I bind all generational curses of iniquity, generational mindsets, and generational hindrances. I bind all satanic harassment that tries to keep me chained to an experience; and unto my psyche, I release the peace of God that surpasses all understanding. I decree and declare that I will love the Lord with all of my heart, mind, and soul. I announce that I'm free to worship God in the beauty of His Holiness.*

SMALL STEPS TO SANITY

4

DEMONSTRATING
the Life
of a Worshipper

> *"They that worship Him must worship Him in spirit and in truth."* (John 4:24)

In the previous chapter, we talked about the heart of a worshipper that God approves, and it was stated that the quality of a person's life depends on the state of his or her heart. Once the heart is right with God, the life will be right. If the heart is sick or sinful, the life can't please God. Now, we want to look at one of the characteristics of the life of a worshipper whose heart is right with the Lord. However, we'll be looking at it from the perspective of worship.

Worship Defined

Of course, worship is more than the time we spend in church to sing solemn songs in adoration to the Lord. True worship starts with your life—it's a lifestyle that manifests the will and love of God in every area of your life.

For the purpose of this book, we want to limit ourselves to that solemn and reverential adoration to God, which must flow from your being. That is, an act of love wherein we pour our heart to God in celebrating who He is to us, on a personal level. It usually involves the sacrifice of praise, which is blessing God for who He is, and thanksgiving, which is blessing God for what He's done. At a higher level, worship is your obedience or allegiance to God.

Worship Translates Our Love for God

The first instance of worship mentioned in the Bible is

found in Genesis 22:5 when Abraham and his son Isaac went up the mountain to worship before God. This act of "worship" meant to bow down or lay prostrate [*face down*] in reverence to the Lord. It was an act of obeisance, or submission and respect.

Let's reiterate that the heart of a worshipper must be pure—right with God. The intent of your heart must be unadulterated, uncontaminated, untainted, unpolluted, uncorrupted, clean, and virtuous. Worship is an extension of your physical being. Worship extends beyond your bodily form and takes you up to the heavenlies. Worship transcends the physical realm and takes you into eternity with God. When you worship, you worship in eternity (*spirit, time without end*) and truth.

At a deeper level, we could say that worship is intimacy or communion with God and God rejoices in our worship because *"love rejoices in truth"* (1 Corinthians 13:6). In all this, the best way to demonstrate our love for the King is through our obedience, and worship is the most intimate form of obedience. Worship translates our love and obedience for the Most High God into a love language that only He can interpret. Worship has to be personal. It is your personal *offering* to the Lord. It has to be your own. You can't mimic worship. You can't be taught how to worship. You have to *become* WORSHIP. You have to be in the moment, allowing nothing to invade that space in time. You must totally surrender _all_ of yourself—not reserving anything for anyone else or even for a later time.

According to *Nelson's New Illustrated Bible Dictionary*, the word "worship" is reverent devotion and allegiance pledged to God. The word "worship" stems from the Old English word "worthship," which refers to the worthiness or value of the one receiving honor or devotion. In other words, your worship is a demonstration of how much you value your Lord and Savior. Is God worthy of your worship? God commands our worship! 1 Chronicles 16:29 encourages us to worship the Lord in the beauty of holiness. Matthew 4:10 gives the command, *"You shall worship the Lord your God, and Him only shall you serve."* Revelation 19:10 and 22:9 instruct us to "worship God." Think about this — worship or the act of worshipping is mentioned nearly 200 times in the Bible (KJV). Your worship is important to JEHOVAH!

Benefits of Worship

When you come before the presence of the King to worship, there are certain benefits you enjoy. Nothing is as good as being a woman or man of God's presence, a person after God's heart. If you knew how much you lost by not going often to the "ivory palace," to worship the King, you would have changed your mentality about worship. It would no longer be a routine, but enjoyable and refreshing moment with God.

Here the graces God has for you if only you will come before His presence in worship:

1. **Impartation of joy**. According to Psalm 16:11, *"in the presence of the Lord is the fullness*

[completeness, richness] of joy and at His right hand are pleasures forevermore." Joy is not the same as happiness, because happiness is a condition of happenstance *[accident, coincidence, chance, circumstance]*—it is short-lived. This joy can only be found in His presence and it keeps bubbling within you regardless of your environment or circumstances.

2. **Infinite pleasure.** When you are in God's presence, you have *eternal* access [24 hour per day/7 days per week/365 days per year] to have and enjoy whatever your heart desires (See Psalm 16:11; 37:4).

3. **Infusion of strength.** The joy of the Lord is a source of strength (See Nehemiah 8:10). Our worship and celebration of the King infuses us with strength. This "strength" is our defense and protection.

4. **Impregnated with the love of Christ and the fullness of God.** As we worship, the King, we come to know [be fully aware of] the love of Christ and we are filled with the fullness of God (See Ephesians 3:14-19).

-------------------------- ♦ --------------------------

Daily Exercises for Worship:

1. Spend time alone with God every day. Set aside at least one hour a day to get in the presence of God. Create

an atmosphere to worship the King. Light some candles, pour yourself a glass of sparkling cider, and, if it won't be a distraction to you (though it all depends on how you have developed your mind for concentration), play soft music while studying the word of God. Or, run a warm scented bubble bath and relax for 30 minutes while meditating on a scripture. Take a 30-minute power-walk during your lunch break while rejoicing in the day that the Lord has made and giving God praise and glory for His wondrous works.

2. Spend time in prayer. Prayer is a fundamental part of worship. Set your clock 30 minutes to an hour earlier than the time of your family altar, so that you can pray before your husband and the children wake up.

3. Journal your acts of worship. In what way have you shown the King how much He is worth to you? What acts of submission and obedience have you performed? How many times in one month have you been disobedient, intentionally or unintentionally?

Daily Scripture Reading: Genesis 22:5, Deuteronomy 26:10, Joshua 5:14, 1 Chronicles 16:29, Psalm 29:1-2, Psalm 66:1-4, Psalm 86:9, Psalm 95:1-6, Psalm 96:1-9, Psalm 99:5&9, Psalm 132:7, Psalm 138:1-2, Matthew 4:10, John 4:23-24, Ephesians 3:14-19

◆

Daily Prayer: *Father in the name of Jesus, today, I worship you in spirit and in truth. I sing praises unto your name and declare your splendor all day long. Early in the morning, I seek and give glory to your name. You're a great and sovereign God and in a parched land, I thirst for you, crying out with a loud cry and singing praises with my mouth. You are the King of kings and the Lord of Lord and I extol you. How majestic is your name in all the earth. In alignment with Psalm 95:1, I worship and bow down and kneel before the Lord my maker. Thank you for accepting my worship and allowing me to make your name large.*

5

DEALING
with Negative
Emotions

> *I wish above all that thou mayest prosper, and be in health, <u>even as your soul prospers</u>!* (3 John 1:2)

> *Now may the God of peace...<u>make you complete</u> in every good work to do His will, working in you what is well pleasing in His sight, through Jesus Christ, to whom be glory forever and ever. Amen.* (Hebrews 13:20-21)

Man is a tripartite being—with spirit, soul, and body. The soul consists of the intellect, passion, desires, and emotions. The enemy desires to attack your emotions with complications, confusion, craziness, and chaos. He knows that we are mostly moved by our feelings, and sometimes our emotions can becloud our mind. Therefore, Satan desires for you to become prisoners of your mind and held hostage by your emotions, so that you can go in circles as on a merry-go-round or going up and down as on a roller coaster. And, he keeps coming at our emotions through what we see, hear, or experience each day.

The enemy wants to keep you defeated through unhealed hurts, unresolved issues, and unmet needs, and by so doing, you will suffer from emotional dysfunction. Understand that when your emotions are negative, you will tend to make decisions based on how you *feel*, rather than the spiritual logic born out of a sound mind.

It's no wonder the thief—the devil himself—comes only to steal, kill, and destroy but Jesus came that you may have life, even more abundantly (John 10:10). God desires for you to be made whole—complete, developed, intact, and lacking nothing—in your whole being. That is God's ideal for your life—Zoë—the God kind of life.

Where the life is, there will be emotional stability, even in the midst of stormy winds that could drive the emotions in the negative direction. If you're emotionally *sick*, you need the Zoë to recover. Herein, you will learn a simple, but powerful approach to your emotional healing today.

Healing from the Inside Out—Completeness

Women, it's time to embrace your healing and to be made whole today! Go has a plan for you, and it's not a function of your feelings but of your mind—you have the mind of Christ. But then, having negative emotions can rob you of a good state of mind, which is required to think the thought of God (Jeremiah 29:11) and align yourself to it. His thought is His will for you, and if care is not taken, your feelings can take you far from it. Once you embrace your healing, you are ready to operate in the will of God.

You will begin to make godly decisions rather than soulish decisions and you will be able to operate in your Kingdom assignment. The state of health of your inner man will always determine your actions or lifestyle. Hebrews 13:20-21 states, "*Now may the God of peace...make you __complete__ in every good work to do His will, working in you what is well pleasing in His sight, through Jesus Christ, to whom be glory forever and ever.*"

It is God's desire for you to be complete (whole) that you may perform His will. It is impossible to operate effectively in the Kingdom with emotional baggage weighing you down. According to Hebrews 12:1 (NIV), *"we are surrounded by such a great cloud of witnesses, let us throw off everything that hinders and the sin that so easily entangles, and let us run with perseverance the race marked out for us."* Women, how can you run with your Kingdom assignment when you are being cumbered with emotional baggage and emotional pitfalls?

Danger of Emotional Pitfalls

People with emotional wounds tend to hurt others, and hurting people tend to view the world through the lenses of offense and hurt. *"To the pure all things are pure, but to the defiled all things are defiled"* (Titus 1:15). You have to walk in healing so that your perception will be pure and not tainted by unhealed hurts, unresolved issues, and unmet needs.

Emotionally scarred people almost always develop unhealthy relationships as a result of and in response to their emotional storms. This is because when you are led by your emotions rather than the Spirit of God, your vision becomes blurred. You are no longer able to discern rightly and you become incapable of making Kingdom decisions. Emotional pitfalls will cause you to forfeit your Kingdom assignment, your destiny, your purpose, and the promises of God.

Practical Steps to Emotional Healing

- **Put on the Full Armor of God!**

God's armor offers protection to your soul—the seat of your intellect, emotions, and will.

> *Finally, be strong in the Lord and in his mighty power. Put on the full armor of God so that you can take your stand against the devil's schemes. For our struggle is not against flesh and blood, but against the rulers, against the authorities, against the powers of this dark world and against the spiritual forces of evil in the heavenly realm. Therefore, put on the full armor of God, so that when the day of evil comes, you may be able to stand your ground, and after you have done everything, to stand. Stand firm then, with the belt of truth buckled around your waist [**Guard your passions!**], with the breastplate of righteousness in place [**Guard/purify your heart!**], and with your feet fitted with the readiness that comes from the gospel of peace [**Keep away from mischief!**]. In addition to all this, take up the shield of faith [**Guard your faith! Keep your confession!**], with which you can extinguish all the flaming arrows of the evil one. Take the helmet of salvation [**Guard your mind/thoughts!**] and sword of the Spirit, which is the **word of God**, and **pray in the Spirit on all occasions** with all kinds of prayers and requests. With this in mind, **be alert** and **always***

keep on praying for all the saints (Ephesians 6:10-18 NIV)

Women, it's time to stand up and fight back! Nevertheless, you first have to arm yourself with the armor of God. Go ahead! Get your joy back! Get your peace back! Get your confidence back! Believe again! Hope again! Dream again! With God on your side, you have all it takes to be what God has called you to be. Don't let anything hold you back. Emotions are nothing more than emotions; keep them at that level since they not the human mind required for logic and reasoning.

- **Increase Your Esteem**

For you created my inmost being; you knit me together in my mother's womb. I praise you because I am fearfully and wonderfully made; your works are wonderful, I know that full well (Psalm 139: 13-15).

Self-esteem is defined as a confidence and satisfaction in oneself. Self-esteem is the total worth or value that you place on your self-image (*your concept of yourself and your role in society*). How you perceive yourself (*your mental image or awareness of yourself*) is very important to how you relate to (*connect, respond, interact with*) yourself and others. What you think of yourself will come across in your behavior, appearance, conversation, and your relationships with others. In order to increase your self-esteem, you must first improve your self-image.

Your self-image is the mental image or awareness of

yourself and your role in society. In other words, your self-image is your perception of what you look like; your level of intelligence; your role or significance in your family, in your community (*church*), in your workplace; what you sound like, etc. What you think about yourself inevitably becomes what you think others think about you, which ultimately determines how you treat or relate to others.

Remember the spies who were sent into Canaan, they saw themselves as grasshoppers and so believed that their enemies saw them as grasshoppers too, and this generated fear—a negative feeling (*Numbers 13:33*). If you place little value on yourself (*low self-respect*), then you will allow others to treat you with little or no regard. People will treat you the way you present yourself to them, and they will judge or value you based on the way you relate with them. Understanding this really becomes significant when applying the biblical principle that says, "*Do unto others as you would have them do unto you.*"

It is impossible to love others if you do not first love yourself. The enemy is after your self-image (*your confidence in and awareness of yourself*). Did you not know that most women around the world have a low self-image? According to a recent study called *The Real Truth about Beauty: A Global Report*, only 2% of women around the world describe themselves as beautiful. If you are frustrated with yourself, then you will relate to others in frustration. If you are angry with yourself, then you will relate to others in anger. If you lack confidence in yourself (your appearance, your intelligence, and/or your significance), then you will allow others to treat you with low regard. But if you love yourself and have confidence in yourself, you can command the respect of others!

Never allow anyone to violate or vandalize you. Never give anyone more power over you than God has. You are worth far more than you may give yourself credit for. In Proverbs 31, a virtuous woman's worth is said to be far above rubies. If you were to research rubies, you would find out that the value of a ruby is determined by the vividness of its rich color and its brilliance. The deep red color of the ruby and its brightness are intensified by heat. Rubies are heated at high temperatures to improve their clarity and to intensify their colors. In other words, your tests, misery, and adversity only serve to increase your value! Another striking fact is that only a diamond-made cutter or another ruby can cut a ruby! It is one of the strongest gems in the earth, next to diamond.

When you think of your self-image, remember that you were fearfully and wonderfully made in the image of the fullness of God! To be fearfully made means to be made with reverence and awe. You are God's creation and His glory on earth! Remember also that God made you to have dominion and to sit down at His right hand along with Jesus Christ, which is a role/position of purpose and importance. God loves us with an everlasting love (Jeremiah 31:3).

Helpful Tips on Emotional Healing

Now, in addition to the two afore-mentioned steps, I would like to give you some other inspiring facts to get along on the journey to your recovery.

- Believe in your *heart* that God will restore your soul, and ask Him to do that. You are required to believe with your heart, not your emotions (Psalm 23:3).

- Set your passion on God, not on man. If you set your emotions on man, you will become disheartened (Psalm 42:1-11). This is where most singles miss it while dating/courting someone. Your heart is too precious to be played upon.

- Cast your cares on God. What led to your hurts or heartache? Why are you depressed today? Let go and let God heal you (Psalm 55:22; 1 Peter 5:7).

- Rest your emotions in God alone. Peradventure, you have just been adopted, jilted, divorced, or fired at your workplace, don't let your feelings cause you a burnout. Look up to God and He will strengthen you and give you a new hope (Psalm 62:5-8).

- Command your emotions to praise God. A spiritual walk with God has nothing to do with feelings but faith. You don't need to feel like it, just praise God. Start with your favorite song today (Psalm 103).

- Believe God will satisfy your soul, for He cares for you (Psalm 107:9).

- Guard your emotions from the wicked. Sometimes, we are hurt by what we hear—based on the way folks address or talk about us—but we must learn to sieve everything that comes to our ears. Prayerfully and mentally, shut out negativity; don't brood over negative things. In addition, stay clear of unhealthy relationship or negative neighbors (Proverbs 22:5).

- Acknowledge that there is healing for your soul in Jesus Christ (Matthew 11:29-30).

- Love God with all your heart, mind, and soul (Matthew 22:37, Mark 12:30).

- Expect God will sanctify you completely (1 Thessalonians 5:23).

- God can heal the brokenhearted; ask Him to heal your heart, too (Luke 4:18; Isaiah 61:1).

- And, for sure, God will comfort you and give you joy (Isaiah 61:2-3).

Daily Exercises for Emotional Healing (Completeness):

- **Emotional Assessment**

1. Are you clothing yourself with your spiritual armor daily? For 30 days, journal the steps you took to clothe yourself with the armor of God.

2. Have you let go of unhealthy people and unhealthy situations? If so, what have you replaced those relationships with in your life? Are you still attaching yourself to unhealthy relationships and circumstances?

3. What doors does the enemy typically come through to stir your emotions? How do you usually react to these situations? Write down your emotional triggers and your reactions. Now write down the actions you can take when you see the enemy trying to come through a familiar door. You must become a woman of action rather than reaction.

- **Self-esteem Assessment**

1. What is your mental image of yourself? Describe yourself. Why do you think that way about yourself?

2. How do you perceive what others think about you? Why do you think that?

_____

_____

3. If you were to place a value on your self-worth, what would your value be? Why?

_____

_____

4. Do you love yourself? Why or why not? What is your definition of love?

_____

_____

5. What do you believe God thinks about you? Why?

_____

_____

———————— ♦ ————————

Daily Scripture Reading (Emotional Assessment):

3 John 2, Hebrews 13:20-21, Titus 1:15, James 5:16, James 1:19-20, Psalm 23:3, Psalm 42:1-11, Psalm 55:22, 1 Peter 5:7, Psalm 62:5-8, Psalm 103, Psalm 107:9, Proverbs 22:5, Matthew 11:29-30, Matthew 22:37, Mark 12:30, 1 Thessalonians 5:23, Luke 4:18, Isaiah 61:1-3

———————— ♦ ————————

Daily Scripture Reading (Self-Esteem Assessment):

Genesis 1:26-31, Genesis 5:1-2, Psalm 8:4-6, Psalm

139:13-14, Isaiah 43:7, 21, Jeremiah 1:5, Ephesians 4:24, Hebrews 2:6-8, 1 John 5:4

---------- • ----------

Daily Prayer: Father in the name of Jesus, I break all generational curses of rebellion, pride, and schizophrenia that will cause me to believe a lie and forfeit the will of God for my life. By the power of your Spirit, I uproot spirits of deep hurts, bitterness, grief, depression, and unforgiveness, and I command them to release my soul in Jesus' name. I forcefully resist the spirit of mental neglect that causes my mind to be in a wandering pattern. I prevail against all satanic harassment that comes in the form of worry, which also brings the spirit of confusion, double-mindedness, forgetfulness, and unbelief. I take on the spirit of a conqueror and stand on the confidence of Philippians 1:6 that God, who has started the good work in me, will complete it. Therefore, Satan, I dismantle your plan and destroy your works. I set my mind on those things, which are lovely, and of good report.

6

DESTROYING
All Demonic Activity
Over Your Head

> *For we wrestle not against flesh and blood, but against principalities, against powers, against the rulers of the darkness of this world, against spiritual wickedness in high places.* (Ephesians 6:12)

It's no secret, and it's no news that we are in a real war with a real devil! If we are ever going to be successful in this war, we have to understand whom we are fighting against, under whose power and authority we are fighting, and the weapons of warfare at our disposal. We have to understand that we *"do not war after the flesh, for the weapons of our warfare are not carnal but they are mighty through God to the pulling down of strongholds"* (2 Corinthians 10:3-4).

Stronghold Defined

What is a stronghold? It is a fortified place ruled by a prince, also known as *principality*. In the Kingdom of Satan, there is a hierarchy of authority among his minions. Therefore, there are different classes of demons at different levels of authority, and it's quite crucial that you are aware of this if you want to win this war. Victory starts with knowing your enemy, his weapons, and his weaknesses. Now, according to Ephesians 6: 10-12, you would find out that the devil has four levels of demonic control in the universe, and they are:

- Principalities
- Powers (demons with special authority)
- Rulers of darkness (ruling spirits over families and regions)

- Spiritual wickedness in high places (idolatry)

All of these evil creatures seek to put us into slavery — in a stronghold. Don't forget that we also must fight against Satan himself, who is our archenemy and the master of the kingdom of darkness. Why is it important to know your enemy? 2 Corinthians 2:11 tells us that we must be aware of the devil's tactics *"lest Satan should get an advantage of us: for we are not ignorant of his devices."* If we don't know whom we're fighting against, then the enemy will have an advantage of us. At worst, you will be fighting your friend, child, spouse, or neighbor. Did they behave abnormally toward you? Look beyond them — someone, *the enemy*, is hiding at their back. Most often, it's not their fault, as they are being manipulated and held hostage in a stronghold.

Weapons at Your Disposal

In this warfare, we have to arm ourselves with the power of God. Apostle Paul in his letter to us tells us to *"be strong in the Lord and in the power of His might."* We fight the battle with His power and under His authority, and not with our own strength. What weapons do we use in this fight? Ephesians 6:10-18 gives us a list of God's provision for victory.

1.   We must be daily equipped with the **armor of God** that we may be able to stand against the wiles (tricks, schemes, strategies) of the devil. God's armor has seven parts, which must be worn as a whole piece — just imagine a Roman soldier.

- First, our passions (our loins) must be girded with the Truth (the word of God). To gird one's loins means to prepare for action. In other words, your emotions, your heart, and your soul must be cleansed through the word of God—always *prepare the heart* for battle as you can't afford to be caught off guard. You have to combat the enemy with the Truth – God's Word. In addition, the *truth belt* is essential to keeping other parts of the armor in place, most especially the breastplate and the sword.

- Second, put on the breastplate of righteousness. Guard your heart with righteousness. Keep your heart pure! If Satan can infect your heart with iniquity or fear, you have already lost the war.

- Third, your feet must be shod with the preparation of the gospel of peace (gospel shoes). The Bible says, *"How beautiful are the feet of those who preach the gospel of peace!"* (Romans 10:15). You must be prepared to preach (declare) God's word wherever you go!

- Fourth, take on the shield of faith. It is your faith in the power and the authority of God that will extinguish the fiery attacks of the enemy. The devil is not after you, he is after your faith in God and in God's word. If he succeeds, he's got you down.

- Fifth, take on the helmet of salvation! The helmet of salvation guards your mind. When you are saved, you must be transformed by the constant renewing of your mind (Romans 12:2; Ephesians 4:23).

- Sixth, take on the sword of the Spirit, which is the word of God, for it is quick, and powerful, and sharper than any two-edged sword. (Hebrews 4:12).

- Seventh, pray always in the Spirit. If you don't want to fall into the trap of the Tempter, you must watch and pray. Remember in Acts 16, Paul and Silas, while they were behind bars, prayed and sang praises unto God and suddenly, the prison doors were opened, and everyone's bands were loosed. Not only were they freed from their bondage but also the keeper of the prison fell down before them asking what he was supposed to do to be saved.

2.   Praise is another powerful weapon in your arsenal. Not only is God's word a weapon, but also our praise is a weapon. Read Psalm 149. Chronicles 20:21-23 tells us that when the children of Israel began to sing praises unto the Lord in the beauty of holiness, the Lord sent a deadly ambush against their enemies.

As mothers, wives, women of God, we must take our place in this war! We have to be mourning women. We have to be cunning women. (Jeremiah 9:17-18). Cunning means to display keen insight; to be skilled, crafty in the use of special resources; or to attain an end. Our special resource is prayer, praise, and declaring the word of

God! The end that we want to attain is victory over the enemy in our ministry, home, career, marriage, businesses, and relationships.

We have to set watch *(night watches)* and pray against the activity of the enemy! We have to know that God has already equipped us with *"power to tread over serpents and scorpions and over all the power of the enemy and nothing shall by any means harm us"* (Luke 10:19). We must also understand that we are not fighting this war alone, for God backs us up. Jeremiah 50:25 says that the Lord has opened his armory and has brought forth the weapons of his indignation, for this is the work of the Lord God of hosts! In other words, you won't even have to fight some battles, because God has said, "Just because you gave me a praise, this battle is on me! I'll fight for you!" (2 Chronicles 20:15-18).

The Price of Victory

Remember that Jesus already disarmed Satan's kingdom when He died on the cross. He spoiled principalities and powers, made them an open shame, and triumphed over them (Colossians 2:15). On that cross, Christ's blood was shed as the price required to purchase all you will ever need in your lifetime. This event means three things for you:

1. No weapon formed against you shall prosper (See Isaiah 54:17).

2. The gates of hell will not prevail over you (See Matthew 16:18).

3. When the enemy shall come against you like a flood, the Spirit of the Lord shall lift up a standard against him (See Isaiah 59:16-19).

100% victory over the enemy is yours. So, put on strength, you women of Zion! (See Isaiah 51:9, 52:1-3). Your warfare is accomplished! (See Isaiah 40:2).

The Major Battleground

Strip yourselves of your former nature [put off and discard your old un-renewed self] which characterized your previous manner of life and becomes corrupt through lusts and desires that spring from delusion; And be constantly renewed in the spirit of your mind [having a fresh mental and spiritual attitude], And put on the new nature (the regenerate self) created in God's image, [Godlike] in true righteousness and holiness (Ephesians 4:22-24)

Do not be conformed to this world (this age), [fashioned after and adapted to its external, superficial customs], but be transformed (changed) by the [entire] renewal of your mind [by its new ideals and its new attitude], so that you may prove [for yourselves] what is the good and acceptable and perfect will of God, even the thing which is good and acceptable and perfect [in His sight for you] (Romans 12:2)

It All Began at Eden

The greatest spiritual warfare for the believer and

particularly for women is warfare in the mind. Eve's first challenge in the Garden of Eden was brought by a question posed in the mind by Satan, "*Yea, hath God said, 'Ye shall not eat of every tree of the garden?'*" (Genesis 3:1-6). The fact that the woman "saw" that the 'forbidden fruit' was good for food was an indication that she entertained the question that Satan posed to her mind. The word "saw" in this sense means to perceive the meaning of, to become aware of, to imagine as a possibility, to form a mental picture of, or to visualize something. In other words, Eve imagined and visualized the possibility that the tree was good for something and then questioned God's command that the tree was forbidden. Maybe she was only trying to help man, Adam. After all, she was created to be a helpmeet to the man. One thing is certain, she was unaware of Satan's devices and did not realize that Satan was waging a spiritual warfare, and the battleground was in the mind! Eve did not realize that she had an opponent—an enemy. She did not know that she had to guard her mind!

Ephesians 6:11-17 tells us to put on the whole armor of God, and one of the pivotal pieces of the armor is the helmet of salvation. As born-again believers, we are transformed by the renewal of our mind and we must be constantly renewed in the spirit of our mind. Salvation allows us to take on a new mind—the mind of Christ. This means we have to put on a new spiritual attitude. We must bring every thought and imagination that comes against the truth of God's word into captivity to the obedience of Christ (2 Corinthians 10:5). Every thought must be subject to the word of God.

My pastor and husband, Pastor Travis Jennings, always says that we must avoid "stinking thinking." We must be like Paul in the face of distress while he was standing trial before King Agrippa—we must think ourselves happy (See Acts 26:2). We must control our thoughts of death (when your promise or dream seems to die in your lap), delays (a delayed promise), distress, and disappointments. When we think of putting on a new mindset, we must think of it as adopting a completely new world—a new way of thinking, a new "fantastic point of view," a new visualization, a new awareness, a clean slate, and a whole new set of possibilities to imagine.

God is not the author of confusion, but He is the author of peace (See 1 Corinthians 14:33). If you entertain any thought that goes against God's written or spoken words, then you are in a state of confusion. Not only are you in a state of confusion but also you are in a state of perversion because anything that is the opposite of the truth of God is perverted. Satan wants to blind the minds of God's people, as revealed in 2 Corinthians 4:4, which says, *"In whom the god of this world hath blinded the minds of them which believe not, lest the light of the glorious gospel of Christ, who is the image of God, should shine unto them."* If Satan can get you to stop believing in God and His word, he will be successful in impeding the *essence* of the gospel of Christ, which is to illuminate the whole being for salvation and a new walk with the Lord.

The Law of the Mind

As women, we have to learn how to stop thinking, stop analyzing, and stop entertaining every thought or question posed by the enemy but we have to accept the will of God and God's word as it is. We may not understand it initially, but we will understand it in God's timing. Eve did not understand why she was forbidden from eating the fruit of the tree of knowledge of good and evil, but it was not for her to understand. She was simply to obey God's command and because of her "stinking thinking," which caused her **not** to be able to judge and discern rightly, she disobeyed God and suffered the consequences.

We must become like the Proverbs 31 woman, the Titus 2:5 woman, and the Proverbs 14:1 woman. We cannot afford to lose the battle in our minds. Proverbs 23:7 says, *"For as a man thinketh in his heart so is he."* Whatever you continually think on, meditate upon, or ponder over will permeate the heart, and you will become what you think! The mind controls every action of the body. Whatever your mind thinks, your body will act upon. Have you ever thought about being sick and you actually began to feel sick? Or, have you ever imagined your favorite dessert and your mouth began to salivate as if you could actually taste it? That's how powerful a thought is! Your mind determines who you are, how you live, and what you will become.

If we as women can discipline our minds to focus on the promises of God, just imagine how different our lives would be. Just imagine the possibilities that we could achieve and accomplish if we think on good things, pure things, honest things, etc. (Philippians 4:8).

You must keep in mind that the law of sin, which rules in your flesh, will always be at war with the spirit of your mind, which is why it is so important to win the war in your mind! If you lose the battle over the war in your mind, then you will become a prisoner to sin. *"But I see another law in my members, warring against the law of my mind, and bringing me into captivity to the law of sin which is in my members"* (Romans 7:23).

We must come to the full knowledge of God, casting down negative thoughts and submitting our will—a part of the soul—to the will of God. If we fail to come to the knowledge of God, God will give us over to a reprobate mind.

"Ever learning, and never able to come to the knowledge of the truth. Now as Jannes and Jambres withstood Moses, so do these also resist the truth: men of corrupt minds, reprobate concerning the faith. But they shall proceed no further: for their folly shall be manifest unto all men, as theirs also was" (2 Timothy 3:7-9).

"And so, since they did not see fit to acknowledge God or approve of Him or consider Him worth the knowing, God gave them over to a base and condemned mind to do things not proper or decent but loathsome" (Romans 1:28).

Winning the Warfare in the Mind

I would like to give you some steps to winning the battle

the enemy is waging against us at the level of the psyche through our thoughts and imaginations. The devil likes to inject words—in the form of thoughts and imaginations—into our mind, to manipulate us into disobedience or rebellion against God's will.

1. We must keep our minds focused steadfastly on God.

> Isaiah 26:3 (AMP) says, *"You will guard him and keep him in perfect and constant peace whose mind [both its inclination and its character] is stayed on You, because he commits himself to You, leans on You, and hopes confidently in You."*

2. Our thoughts should be pure.

> *And the peace of God, which passeth all understanding, shall keep your hearts and minds through Christ Jesus. Finally, brethren, whatsoever things are true, whatsoever things are honest, whatsoever things are just, whatsoever things are pure, whatsoever things are lovely, whatsoever things are of good report; if there be any virtue, and if there be any praise, think on these things* (Philippians 4:7-8).

3. We must gird the loins of our minds in obedience. We must prepare our minds for action with obedience to the word of God.

> *So brace up your minds; be sober (circumspect, morally alert); set your hope wholly and unchangeably on the grace (divine favor) that is coming to you when Jesus Christ (the Messiah) is revealed. [Live] as*

*children of obedience [to God]; do not conform
yourselves to the evil desires [that governed you] in
your former ignorance [when you did not know the
requirements of the Gospel]* (1 Peter 1:13-14, AMP).

4. We must have a Christ-like mind! We must be willing
to have a mind transfer—we must exchange our carnal,
negative, and impure thoughts for new, positive
thoughts and a renewed mind. For every negative
thought that comes to your mind, you must replace it
with the word of God!

> *"Let this mind be in you, which was also in Christ
> Jesus"* (Philippians 2:5).

5. We must serve God with our mind.

> *"I thank God through Jesus Christ our Lord. So then
> with the mind I myself serve the law of God; but with
> the flesh the law of sin"* (Romans 7:25).

6. We must glorify God with our mind.

> *"That ye may with one mind and one mouth glorify
> God, even the Father of our Lord Jesus Christ"*
> (Romans 15:6).

> *And at the end of the days [seven years], I,
> Nebuchadnezzar, lifted up my eyes to heaven, and my
> understanding and the right use of my mind returned
> to me; and I blessed the Most High [God] and I praised
> and honored and glorified Him Who lives forever,
> Whose dominion is an everlasting dominion; and His
> kingdom endures from generation to generation*
> (Daniel 4:34 AMP).

> *Because when they knew and recognized Him as God, they did not honor and glorify Him as God or give Him thanks. But instead they became futile and godless in their thinking [with vain imaginings, foolish reasoning, and stupid speculations] and their senseless minds were darkened* (Romans 1:21 AMP).

——————— • ———————

Exercises for Spiritual Warfare:

Self-Assessment on Spiritual Warfare

1. Describe the spiritual warfare you are facing. What are you doing to counter the attacks of the enemy?

_____

_____

2. Create a study journal. In your study journal, write down key scriptures that ministered to you or write down the revelation God gave you concerning His word as you study. How many hours per day or per week did you study this month?

_____

_____

3. Create a prayer journal. What or who do you focus on most in prayer (ministry, family, finances, etc.)? How many hours per day did you pray?

_____

_____

Self-Assessment on the Battle of the Mind

1. Describe the mental warfare you are facing. What do you find yourself thinking the most about?

_____

_____

2. What are you doing to counteract the warfare in your mind? What are you replacing the negative thoughts with?

_____

_____

◆

Daily Scripture Reading (Warfare & Weapons):

Ephesians 6:10-18; 1 Peter 2:2-3; 1 Timothy 4:15; Hebrews 6:1; 2 Peter 1:5-8; Ephesians 3:14-19; Colossians 1:9-11; 2 Corinthians 3:18; Philippians 1:6, 9-10; Ephesians 4:14-15; 1 Peter 4:12-16

◆

Daily Scripture Reading (Battle of the Mind): Ephesians 4:22-24, Romans 12:2, Ephesians 6:11-17, 2 Corinthians 10:5, Acts 26:2, 1 Corinthians 14:33, 2 Corinthians 4:4, Proverbs 23:7, Romans 7:23-25, Isaiah 26:3, Philippians 4:7-8, 1 Peter 1:13-14, Philippians 2:5, Romans 15:6, Daniel 4:34, Romans 1:21

Small Steps to Sanity

Daily Prayer: *Father in the name of Jesus, I take the earth by its edges and shake wickedness out of it. I thank you for the key of David that grants us all access I need, so now I come boldly before the throne of grace. I pull down every stronghold of fear, poverty, lawlessness, and prayerlessness. I bind the strongman, spoil his goods, and render him helpless. I bind all principalities, powers, rulers of darkness of this world, and spiritual wickedness in high places. I put on the full armor of God and stand during the day of attack and adversity. I decree and declare, because of this agreement, that those who are prisoners of their soul be loosed. I stand on the confidence of Psalms 62:1 that power belongs to God. You are my strength and I sing praises to you, because you are my fortress and strong tower. I rejoice knowing that the greater One lives on the inside of me. And if God be for me, who can be against me?*

SMALL STEPS TO SANITY

7

DESTROYING
the Myth about Women
and Relationships

> *"For whosoever shall do the will of my Father which is in heaven, the same is my brother, and **sister**, and mother"* (Matthew 12:50).

The body of Christ is made up of different parts working together for a common goal. Individually, we all have a relationship with the Father, and there is a *bond* we have with one another, too. In your journey as a Christian woman, you need others to survive, and you are called to help others grow or develop in their spiritual walk.

It's high time women came together to further the cause of the gospel, to promote "Sisterhood" in today's Church. We can't afford to be isolated from one another; let's begin to reconnect with one another.

Now, are you your sister's keeper? Yes you are! What is *Sisterhood*? A sisterhood is a collaboration of women sharing common goals and interests, being <u>united</u> for a common cause. This bond is as a three-fold cord, which cannot be easily broken.

The Weakness of a Woman

One problem that is often prevalent within a large group or family of women is contention. Women tend to be catty, competitive, and covetous rather than encouraging, empowering, and enriching. They tear each other down rather than lift one another up. I call this the "crab" spirit. Women, particularly the idle ones, are oftentimes the source of gossip and strife.

Women also tend to form cliques, which exclude a certain group of people —those they don't like to be with. Aren't you tired of the cliché that women cannot work together or that women cannot get along with each other?

> *Behold, how good and pleasant it is when brothers dwell in unity! It is like the precious oil on the head, running down on the beard, on the beard of Aaron, running down on the collar of his robes! It is like the dew of Hermon, which falls on the mountains of Zion! For there the LORD has commanded the blessing, life forevermore.* (Psalm 133)

In other words, it is at the place of unity (*the connection point*) that the Lord commands His blessing eternally such that we are restored, refreshed, and reinvented. Women, let's look inward and address all those weaknesses that often position us against God's fullness of grace, elegance, and glory. All our character flaws, which make us pissed off at one another, should be dealt with, so that we can work as a formidable force on earth. There is a reason for being female as far as God's agenda for humanity and the Church is concerned. Don't let anything deprive you of God's purpose for creating you in the first place.

The Power of a Woman

As soon as we put our differences behind, and turn our weaknesses to strengths, we can build others up. The best thing in life is to make a difference in someone's life. God created you to be an impact maker everywhere you go. You can't just live for yourself alone—you must live for others as well.

The Bible—the Word of God—has many things to tell us regarding His expectations from us:

- As women of God, we should be able to exhort one another in love and purity. John 13:35 (AMP) says, *"By this shall all [men] know that you are My disciples, if you love one another [if you keep on showing love among yourselves]."*

- Proverbs 17:17 says, *"A friend loveth at all times, and a brother is born for adversity."* As sisters in Christ, we should be able to encourage and uplift one another during difficult situations.

- Romans 12:10 (AMP) tells us to *"love one another with brotherly affection [as members of one family], giving precedence and showing honor to one another."*

- 1 Timothy 5:2 (AMP) says that we should *"treat older women like mothers [and] younger women like sisters, **in all purity**."*

In every respect, women should be able to love one another with a pure heart and mind without malice, jealousy, envy, contention, or strife. Before we can connect with one another as women in Christ, we first need to have our hearts purified and our minds renewed.

Women have the power, influence, and ability to change a nation and advance the Kingdom of God. Women were called upon to cry out and pray for the nation in Jeremiah 9:17-18. It thus suggests that women have the ability to birth out a move of God. Hannah birthed out

Samuel, a prophet, when there was no open vision in the land. Day and night, Anna gave herself to prayer and fasting at the temple, interceding for Israel on the coming Messiah. Mary Magdalene, the woman with the alabaster box of precious ointment, prepared Jesus' body for burial.

The Prophetic Destiny of a Woman

Women, you are dreamers. A **D.R.E.A.M** is a Divinely Revealed Event Awaiting Manifestation. It's been noted earlier on that women can birth out God's plan on earth; they can act as the vessel or channel through which a specific intent in God's mind comes into a tangible reality. Check your Bible; you will find out that this is true of all women. God made it that way! At least, for instance, you may not be in a gospel ministry, but you're the vessel that gives birth to destinies.

Jesus came through Virgin Mary; the baby in your womb is a bundle of divine purpose waiting for manifestation. Therefore, you have a D.R.E.A.M!

You may not be the next Virgin Mary, but you can be a Sarah, Deborah, Ruth, Hannah, or Anna. If women are to walk into their manifestation as Dreamers, they must become women of *action*, *agreement*, and *acceleration*.

1. Action

James 1:25 (MSG) says, *"But whoever catches a glimpse of the revealed counsel of God—the free life!—even out of the corner of his eye, and sticks with it, is no distracted scatterbrain but a man or woman of action. That person will find delight and affirmation in the action."*

However, as women of action, we must stay in Attack Mode. That is, you must pick up a fight in your spirit. Recall that we have spiritual warfare around us—we can't sit on the fence. This means we must take aggressive actions against the enemy forces, using our weapons of mass destruction to counterattack and cancel every plan and booby trap that the enemy has set up against our emotions, mind, marriage, finances, household, children, career, and destiny. The only way we can achieve this is to engage in *Prophetic Prayer, Prophetic Praise,* and *Prophetic Words.*

- **What is Prophetic Prayer?** Prophetic prayer is when you pray and counteract the plan of the enemy before it happens.

- **What is Prophetic Praise?** This is when you praise God in advance by faith on the promises of God, with the assurance that it's already done. You have to walk by divine revelation (*faith*) not by feeling or physical appearance (*sight*). You must have an assurance in the character, ability, strength, and truth of God's word.

- **What are Prophetic Words?** Prophetic words are prophetic confessions. Proverbs 18:21 says, *"Death and life is in the power of the tongue; and they that love it shall eat the fruit thereof."* Romans 4:17b also tells us to *"calleth those things that be not as though they are."*

2. Agreement

As women of action, we must stay in Agreement Mode. This means we must always be in one accord, in harmony, giving no room or place for the enemy to enter in and bring division. No more cliques! When we are in one accord, with one mind, and in one spirit, nothing can be withheld from us. We can do it better together!

3. Acceleration

As women of action, we must stay in Acceleration Mode. Our momentum should always increase in rate and speed, thus causing us to become progressive, cutting-edge women of action, and avoiding all emotional pitfalls. We must not be sluggish but grow in grace.

The Love of a Woman

Hebrews 10:25 says, *"We should not forsake the assembling of ourselves together, but rather we should exhort one another even more so in the end times."* Aren't you tired of going to church and not having a clue of the sister sitting next to you? We should be concerned about souls and getting connected—building relationships based on Christ's foundation. At the end of each church meeting, greet a sister you've never met before and connect with her. When you dwell in the presence of the Lord, everyone connected to you will receive the overflow of your relationship with Jesus Christ.

Let's look at love through the eyes of Christ, according to John 3:16 (AMP), which says, *"For God so greatly loved and dearly prized the world that He [even] gave up His only begotten (unique) Son, so that whoever believes in (trusts in, clings to, relies on) Him shall not perish (come to destruction, be lost) but have eternal (everlasting) life."* So it's fair to say that love causes one to do two things: *give* and *live.*

God's love for us ran so deep that He had to create 'something' unique to save us from the pit of damnation. He took divinity and wrapped it in humanity (See John 1:14). He's done the same thing in you, for you're a new creation in Christ. I believe that you are a unique creation. Besides, He has poured His love into you. Let's begin to give out the love.

As from today, make a commitment to give someone a smile, a morning salutation, a thank you, or a ride to church (without asking for gas money). Give out of yourself. When you give out of love, people will begin to live because what comes from the heart goes to the heart. Allow others to benefit from the overflow of your love. No more cliques.

Let's get connected to one another with love—a divine bond. *"And above all these things put on charity, which is the bond of perfectness"* (Colossians 3:14).

------------------- ♦ -------------------

Daily Exercises for Connection:

1. Choose one "sister" relationship in your workplace, family, community, or church. Actively and intentionally work on improving that relationship for the next 30 days. How has that relationship changed?

How have you been blessed by improving this "sister relationship"?

_____

_____

2. Think about your relationships with the women in your family. How have these relationships contributed to the negative attitude or behavior you have developed in your current relationships with women? Journal your memories and thoughts. What steps can you take to shift your thinking?

_____

_____

3. Do you have a spiritual "Naomi" or female role model? Who is your role model and why?

_____

_____

———— ♦ ————

Daily Scripture Reading: Hebrews 10:25, John 13:35, Matthew 12:50, Proverbs 17:17, Romans 12:10 [AMP], 1 Timothy 5:2 [AMP], Psalm 133, Matthew 5:16, Isaiah 61:1, John 12:36, Romans 13:12, James 5:16

———— ♦ ————

Daily Prayer: Father God, in the name of Jesus, I pray for the bond of sisterhood, because you said in your word, "by this you will know my disciples by the love they have one for another." I bind the enemy that brings about misunderstandings, confusion, and arguments among women. I bind self-righteousness, separation, and self-sabotage, understanding that no man is an island. I shout with a loud voice, "I AM MY SISTERS' KEEPER!" I decree and declare that today I'll make new kingdom connections and embrace my sisters in Christ.

SMALL STEPS TO SANITY

8

DISCOVERING
Supernatural
Abundance

> *"But thou shalt remember the LORD thy God: for it is he that giveth thee power to get wealth, that he may establish his covenant which he sware unto thy fathers, as it is this day"* (Deuteronomy 8:18)

> *"Now unto Him that is able to do exceeding abundantly above all that we ask or think, according to the power that worketh in us"* (Ephesians 3:20)

When you consider the ministry of Jesus, you would find out that certain women—Mary Magdalene and company—were in charge of the Welfare Department, so to say. Jesus had no moneymaking ventures; these women were there to meet His needs in *cash* and in *kind*. As women, God wants to direct the riches of the earth into our coffer so we can serve God's intent—as a support to our husbands and financiers of the gospel of Christ on earth. Can you be trusted with wealth?

Wealth Defined

Wealth is more than just the state of being rich and having money. Wealth is defined as an abundance of valuable material possessions or resources; abundant supply; an abundance of anything; plentiful amount; prosperity; material comfort; privileged circumstances; valuable content or produce. I think the last two meanings state it best—wealth is determined by the favor of God and the power on the inside of you. "Privileged circumstances" is another way of saying FAVOR! God's favor is more valuable than money.

Valuable content or produce is another term for the creative power to produce on the inside of you! Another key word in the definition of wealth is "abundant" or "abundance." Think about this!

According to John 10:10, Jesus came so that we may have life more abundantly. The word "abundantly" in Greek means superabundant (in quantity); superior (in quality); or advantageous. Therefore, it makes sense that God desires that you live a "SUPERB" life—one that is extraordinary, wonderful, and overflowing.

The Origin of Wealth

Your mindset has a lot to do with your power to possess wealth. According to Napoleon Hill, the author of *Think & Grow Rich*, we are attracted to the forces, people, and circumstances that harmonize with our dominating thoughts. Success and money only come to those who are success-and-money-conscious. Likewise, failure comes to those who are failure-conscious. Whatever the mind of man can conceive and believe, it will achieve. In other words, if you have a poverty mentality, you will live in poverty. But if you have a prosperous mentality, you will become prosperous!

Tapping the Gold—Riches and Wealth

First, we must remember that it is God that gives us the creative power to get wealth. He is our source and He alone supplies our need—not our jobs, our 401(k), or our retirement plans. He is our Shepherd and because He is, we shall not be in want (Psalm 23:1). Secondly, we must remember that wealth is only granted to us for His purpose and not for our selfish motives. Once we understand these two important principles, we are ready to receive and acquire wealth. Now, having understood that God is the source of the creative power that works on the inside of us, we must learn how to tap into and harness that power to work in our favor.

- As I mentioned earlier, your mindset has a lot to do with your power to possess wealth. You must think wealthy. You must think prosperous. You must think success. Fear, failure, and poverty thinking will cancel out your power to create and possess wealth.

- You must also be cognizant of the company you keep. Your network often determines your net worth. If you surround yourself with poverty-minded people, then you will become poverty-minded. Surround yourself with prosperity-minded people who inspire, motivate, and challenge you.

- Next, you must study to show yourself approved (2 Timothy 2:15). Arm yourself with knowledge. The word *"study"* in 2 Timothy 2:15 means to make effort, to be prompt, to endeavor, to be diligent. If you desire to go into business, then study the industry you're trying to break into. Study your craft. Invest in your God-given gifts, talents, and abilities, to learn how to make them work for you. Study the life of other wealthy people. How did they obtain their wealth? How do they maintain their wealth? Learn about finances and investing for your future so that you can be a good and faithful steward over the resources God has given you. Study the word of God concerning wealth and finances. Your diligent effort will determine your level of wealth (Proverbs 10:4).

- You must have a desire mixed with faith. You have not because you ask not. God can only bless to the degree of your desire. He is able to do exceeding abundantly above all that you can ask or think according to the power [desire] that goes to work within you. If you never aspire for anything, you should not expect to achieve anything. John 16:24 says, *"Ask, and ye shall receive, that your joy may be full."* Mark 11:24 says, *"What things soever ye desire, when ye pray, believe that ye receive them, and ye shall have them."*

- You must have a definite plan. How do you plan to become wealthy? What are your spiritual and financial goals for the next 3 months, 6 months, 9 months, 12 months, 15 months, 18 months, 3 years, and 5 years?

  1. You must have a goal to measure yourself against. Your goals must be relevant, realistic (reasonable,

sound), and realizable (reachable, attainable).

2. Your plan should be in writing. Habakkuk 2:2 says, *"Write the vision, and make it plain."*

3. You must Pray, Plan, and Prioritize.

    a. **Pray** – *"Seek ye first the kingdom and His righteousness, and all these things shall be added unto you"* (Matthew 6:33).

    b. **Plan** – *"Commit your ways unto the Lord and your plans will prosper"* (Proverbs 16:3).

    c. **Prioritize** – *"But everything should be done in decency and in order"* (1 Corinthians 14:40).

Purpose of Wealth

A maxim goes thus, 'When the purpose of a thing is not known, abuse is inevitable.' God does not give you wealth for you to hoard your riches and become greedy and selfish. Remember those women that supported Christ's ministry with their resources. Your wealth contains seed and fruit. In my personal view, it is 50-50—50% seed and 50% fruit.

You don't eat the seed with the fruit—sow it into people's lives, charities, foundations, scholarships, your local church, etc. You can't expect to reap a harvest without first sowing a seed.

The Word of God confirms the foregoing facts, as stated below:

- 2 Corinthians 9:6 says, *"He which soweth sparingly shall reap also sparingly; and he which soweth bountifully shall reap also bountifully."*

- Galatians 6:7 says, *"Be not deceived; God is not mocked: for whatsoever a man soweth, that shall he also reap."*

- Luke 6:38 says, *"Give, and it shall be given unto you...For with the same measure that ye mete [to give] withal it shall be measured to you again."*

If you study the richest people in the world, you will find that they are givers or philanthropists. The principle works the same in the Kingdom. If you sow into the Kingdom, the Kingdom will sow back to you!

◆

Daily Exercises for Possessing Wealth:

1. What is your plan to create and possess wealth? Do you have relevant, realistic, and realizable goals? Write down your wealth plan and recite it to yourself every morning and night.

———————————————————

———————————————————

2. Study. What books are you reading? How are you increasing your knowledge tank?

———————————————————

———————————————————

3. Who are your friends, colleagues, or associates? Evaluate each of them. Are your friends success-conscious? Do they have a wealth plan? Are they putting their plan into action? Do they inspire, challenge, or motivate you? Have they achieved anything great recently?

———————————————————

———————————————————

4. Do you have a mentor? If not, find one. Make plans to have lunch with your mentor once or twice a month, to glean from her wisdom.

———————————————————

———————————————————

5. Have you honored the Lord with your wealth according to Proverbs 3:9-10? According to Malachi 3:8-

11, when you sow your tithe and offering unto God, not only will He open up the windows of heaven but He will also rebuke the devourer for your sake!

Daily Scripture Reading:

Deuteronomy 8:18, 2 Chronicles 1:12, Psalm 66:12, Psalm 112:3, Proverbs 13:22, Proverbs 19:4, Ecclesiastes 5:19, Malachi 3:8-11, Mark 11:24, Genesis 26:13, 1 Chronicles 29:12, Proverbs 8:18, Proverbs 10:4, Proverbs 3:9-10, Psalm 49:20, Proverbs 10:22, Proverbs 13:22, Ecclesiastes 5:10, Jeremiah 5:25, Philippians 4:19, Psalm 23:1, 1 John 5:14

Daily Prayer: Father God, let the resurrection power of Jesus Christ come upon the works of my hands and cause an abundance of wealth to flow in my life. Father, it is you who causes me to receive the power, vigor, strength, and spiritual capacity to obtain wealth so that you may establish your covenant in the earth. I pray for the power and anointing to receive wealth and I break every generational curse that has hindered prosperity in my life. As I am obedient to your Word regarding tithes and offerings, I pray for the windows of heaven to open and for an outpouring of blessings so great that I will not have room to receive. I stand in faith today believing for supernatural increase in my finances, Because of my willingness to sow bountifully, I know that I will reap bountifully. I give cheerfully to you Father for the advancement and up building of your kingdom and to also meet the needs of others as you guide me.

SMALL STEPS TO SANITY

9

DEPLOYING
the
New You

> *Arise [from the depression and prostration in which circumstances have kept you – rise to a new life]! Shine (be radiant with the glory of the Lord), for your light has come, and the glory of the Lord has risen upon you!* (Isaiah 60:1)

If you have been following along in this book, you should be on your way to being the very person that God wants you to be. He created you in His likeness, after the image of Christ when you were born again.

If you have religiously followed the Daily Exercises, you have begun to write a brand-new chapter in the history of your life. By now, I want to believe you have uncovered God's purpose for your life, purified your heart, applied the principles of prayer and fasting, engaged yourself in spiritual warfare, and successfully conquered the warfare in your mind.

Moreover, your self-esteem has increased, and you have completed your transformation with healing.

Now you are ready to transition into your new era — your defining moment! Recall that adversities of life offer you a refining moment so that you can transition into your defining moment wherein you find a real expression for whom you are in God. Your uniqueness and identity is defined with a purpose.

Refining Moment — *a time in which the believer, though tried and tested, perseveres with unwavering stamina and great perseverance.*

> *Defining Moment* — *a time in which the*
> *believer comes out pure as gold after having*
> *patiently passed through the refining moment.*

A moment is a point in time; an instant; a time of success, excellence, importance and influence; a cause of action; a stage in historical development. When you embrace your defining moment, you are making history. When you embrace your defining moment, you can influence and shape a nation. Your defining moment will leave a lasting imprint on your generation!

A moment can also be defined as a juncture, which is not only a point in time, but also a transition [an evolutionary and pivotal shift in time]. It is the result of an agreement and a coming together of events in time. No matter how tough your experience might be now, God is getting ready to align everything in your favor for your defining moment to occur.

Many people walk in fear of embracing their refining and defining moments because they fail to come into the full knowledge of God's word. 2 Peter 1:3 says, *"According as his divine power hath given unto us all things that pertain unto life and godliness, through the knowledge of him that hath called us to glory and virtue."* Glory means splendor, magnificence, and brilliance. Virtue means having a high quality, value, or caliber; a desirable quality. In other words, God has called us to shine and to live a high quality, high caliber life. However, instead of embracing the truth of God's word, most women believe the lie, the false image that the devil has placed before them, *or* that they have placed before themselves.

Attributes of the New You

In order to actualize your new **you**, you will need *fortitude, faith*, and *favor*.

1. Fortitude

You must put on strength. You must have a strong mental attitude to endure pain and adversity with courage. You must overcome **fear** to walk into this new era of your life. And, don't forget those facts you have learned about the human mind. The quality of your life is determined by the state of your mind.

> *"Thou wilt keep him in perfect peace, whose mind is stayed on thee: because he trusteth in thee"* (Isaiah 26:3).

> *"And be constantly renewed in the spirit of your mind [having a fresh mental and spiritual attitude"* (Ephesians 4:23).

> *"Let this mind be in you, which was also in Christ Jesus"* (Philippians 2:5).

> *"Therefore, prepare your minds for action; be self-controlled; set your hope fully on the grace to be given you when Jesus Christ is revealed"* (1 Peter 1:13 NIV).

> *"Let us not become weary in doing good, for at*

> *the proper time we will reap a harvest if we do not give up"* (Galatians 6:9 NIV).

> *"For God hath not given us the spirit of fear; but of power, and of love, and of a sound mind"* (2 Timothy 1:7).

Fear implies anxiety and loss of courage; reluctance to face a person or situation; a distressing emotion aroused by the threat of impending danger, whether the threat is real or imagined. You can spend a lifetime in fear of something imagined, something that was never real.

Fear is an emotional response. But God has given us a calm, well-balanced, disciplined mind with self-control. Now that you have transformed your mind and you are healed emotionally, you can control your emotional responses. Don't allow anything to keep you paralyzed in fear, or prevent you from your new era, or keep you from your "defining moment."

Our former First Lady, Eleanor Roosevelt, once said, "You gain strength, courage, and confidence by every experience in which you really stop to look fear in the face." You must do the thing that you _think_ you cannot do. Stop telling yourself that you can't do it and Just Do It! Sometimes you are your biggest hindrance.

2. Faith

Mark 4:40 says, *"Why are ye so fearful? How is it that ye have no faith?"* Have faith in God!

Faith is a strong trust and confidence in the invisible God, to cause invisible things to materialize. According to Hebrews 11:1 in the Message Bible translation, *"Faith is the firm foundation that makes life worth living. It's our handle on what we cannot see."*

These are some biblical facts to note on faith:

- **Your faith will come alive when coupled with good works.** James 2:17 (AMP) says, *"So also faith, if it does not have works (deeds and actions of obedience to back it up), by itself is destitute of power (inoperative, dead)."*

- **Your faith has conquering power.** *"For whatsoever is born of God overcometh the world: and this is the victory that overcometh the world, even our faith"* (1 John 5:4).

- **Your faith has speaking power.** *"For verily I say unto you, That whosoever shall say unto this mountain, Be thou removed, and be thou cast into the sea; and shall not doubt in his heart, but shall believe that those things which he saith shall come to pass; he shall have whatsoever he saith"* (Mark 11:23).

- **Your faith gives you walking power.** *"It's what we trust in but don't yet see that keeps us going. We walk by divine revelation and not physical appearance"* (2 Corinthians 5:17 MSG).

3. Favor

You must understand that as you enter into your new season, the favor of God is upon you, and God's grace will see you through.

> *"For his anger endureth but a moment; in his favour is life: weeping may endure for a night, but joy cometh in the morning"* (Psalm 30:5).

> *"By this I know that you favor and delight in me, because my enemy does not triumph over me"* (Psalm 41:11).

> *"Thou shalt arise, and have mercy upon Zion: for the time to favour her, yea, the set time, is come"* (Psalm 102:13).

> *"In the light of the king's countenance is life; and his favour is as a cloud of the latter rain"* (Proverbs 16:15).

Attributes of the New Era

God does not only heal and renew you, but also He gives you a new beginning, a new season. In this new era of your life, get ready for *Divine Intervention*, *Divine Order*, and *Divine Timing*.

> **Divine Intervention:** Heaven is going to intervene in your earthly matters; you will be at peace while God takes your case upon Himself and His Angels.

> **Divine Order:** Heaven is going to give an

authoritative command, direction or instruction concerning your life. God will order your steps and cause everything to come into alignment with His will for your life—all things will work together for your good.

God will command both angels and man to bless you. He will divinely orchestrate and connect you with the people who have the power, the influence, and the ability to help you!

Divine Timing: God will cause all things to align with the time that Heaven has planned, prearranged, and made ready to move events and people on your behalf. Heaven will suspend rules or protocols to bless you.

In all this, you have to stop living in the past—the past is past. You're new now. Now it is time to walk into your new era and be *you*—in a new way!

---- ◆ ----

Daily Exercises for Welcoming Your New Era:

1. Prepare yourself for your new era. If you have been journaling, go back and read over what you have discovered about yourself. When you ignore your past, you are doomed to repeat it.

Confession brings healing and deliverance. Confess your past faults and tell yourself you are no longer that person. Then confess who you are now.

2. Write down the plans and goals you want to accomplish in your new era. Then write down the main excuses you might give yourself that could keep you from the pursuit of your goals. Lastly, write down what steps you can take to counter the excuses you might give yourself.

3. Load yourself with scriptures to meditate on concerning your new era and the new *you*.

———————— ◆ ————————

Daily Scripture Reading

Ecclesiastes 3:1, Daniel 2:21, Proverbs 3:5-6, Psalm 119:105, Psalm 30:5, Psalm 41:11, Psalm 102:13, Proverbs 16:15, 2 Corinthians 5:17, Mark 11:23, 1 John 5:4, James 2:17, Hebrews 11:1, Mark 4:40, 2 Timothy 1:7, Galatians 6:9, 1 Peter 1:13, Philippians 2:5, Ephesians 4:23, Isaiah 26:3, 2 Peter 1:3, Isaiah 60:1

Daily Prayer: Father in the name of Jesus, I put you in charge of my work, so that my plans can take place. God, give me true intelligence that springs up like freshwater

Small Steps to Sanity

and overflows like a river. I thank you for your gracious speech like clovers honey, which is good for the soul and gives life to the body. I decree and declare that my purpose is not confusion, my potential is not bondage, and my destiny is not in chaos. Give me strength to bring forth my destiny. God, help me to know your word, speak your word, and demonstrate your word in my everyday lives. I announce that multiplicity is upon me and I walk in a plethora of blessings. I thank you for divine wisdom and witty invention and I decree that the thoughts in my head will become the wealth to bring forth manifested promises.

ABOUT THE AUTHOR

Dr. Stephanie Jennings serves as co-laborer with her husband, Apostle Travis Jennings to lead the Harvest Tabernacle Church in metro Atlanta. As the senior leaders, together they have pastored a progressive, radical, thriving, bible teaching, apostolic, prophetic, multi-racial, and mission-driven church for the past 15 years. Pastor Stephanie is one of the most prominent leading ladies in Atlanta. As a sought after speaker, she is a kingdom leader, prophetic life coach, successful author, shrewd entrepreneur, prosperity provoker, a philanthropist and a passionate mentor to women and girls. God has called Pastor Stephanie not only to serve in her local church, but to help other leading ladies learn the ultimate balancing act between their domestic life (home and family) and their divine life (ministry and business) and to be effective in both. She accomplishes this through several key initiatives that allow her to personally connect with other leading ladies and share the tools of wisdom she has mastered. As a kingdom trailblazer, Pastor Stephanie launched her Pretty Chics Collection clothing line in 2014. Created to positively impact the self-esteem and self-perception in all women, Pastor Stephanie has revolutionized the Christian Community with the Pretty Chics Movement. Through this platform, she encourages women everywhere to embrace their total body – campaigning that beauty extends from the inside out. She inspires all with her mantra, "love the You—that God has created!" Pastor Stephanie also hosts "Mocha Monday" a weekly prayer line, initiated to empower participants (regionally and nationally) each Monday morning. She believes that "if you speak to the top of your week, God will manifest the rest of your week." Her loving partnership with her very own king, priest and husband, Apostle Travis Jennings, serves as a model for marriages around the world. They have five beautiful children Travis, Briona, Daja, Destiny and David Christopher.

CONTACT INFORMATION

The Harvest Tabernacle Church
1450 South Deshon Road
Lithonia, GA 30058
tsjbookings@gmail.com
www.theharvesttabernacle.org